Creating a Learning Climate for the Early Childhood Years

by
Carol B. Hillman

Library of Congress Catalog Card Number 89-61963
ISBN 0-87367-292-5
Copyright © 1989 by the Phi Delta Kappa Educational Foundation
Bloomington, Indiana

This fastback is sponsored by the Fordham University Chapter of Phi Delta Kappa, which made a generous contribution toward publication costs.

The chapter sponsors this fastback in recognition of the 20th anniversary of the chapter's founding in November 1969.

Table of Contents

Introduction 7

The Early Childhood Scene 9

A Learning Climate for Young Children 11

The Teacher's Role in Creating a Positive Learning Climate 13

The First Few Days of School: Making the Transition 17

Creating a Positive Climate in the Classroom 18

The Classroom Out-of-Doors 22

School Climate and Staff Interaction 24

Working with Parents to Create a Positive Learning Climate 26
    Parent Orientation 27
    The Parent Conference 31

Conclusion 33

Introduction

The education of our young children is in a tumultuous state. There are many reasons for this condition. The world has become a more complex place in which to live. Our systems of communication have quickened. We are given more information to process. We are in touch with problems of nations and problems of people throughout the world. We have much with which to contend. The speed of our lives has accelerated; we are scheduled and over-scheduled. There appears to be little time for repose.

The pressures of society experienced by adults filter down to our children. They, too, seem to have less time for repose, less time for childhood, less time to explore and discover the natural world, less time to just play, less time to dream. As responsible adults we need to grapple with these pressures. We need to moderate our own pace of living. We need to discover the beauty of the world that lies around us. As responsible adults we need to find our own repose.

As responsible educators and parents, we need to take a hard look at the pressures in our society that are affecting the early childhood years. We need to ask what is important in the life of young children. We need to ask ourselves what our priorities are and how we should best go about achieving them. We need to become aware of what needs to be done and what needs to be undone. We each need to act out of our own resolve to remove young children from the tumult – and still find time for our own repose. We need to provide them with an environnment where optimum, age-approporiate learning can take place.

This is what this fastback is about — creating a rich and nurturing learning climate for the early childhood years.

The Early Childhood Scene

One of the alarming trends taking place in early childhood today is the tendency of young parents to provide too much too soon for their youngsters. Infants are enrolled in swimming classes before their bodies can accommodate the stress that is placed on them. Toddlers are taken to gymnastics class and subjected to exercises before they have mastered the skills of running, skipping, and jumping. Small children with no particular musical inclination are pressured to learn the violin. Four-year-olds are being tutored so that they will test well in order to gain entrance to the "right" kindergarten. Pushed by overly ambitious parents, these so-called "hot house tots" are expected to perform and excel in activities that are beyond their physical and emotional capabilities.

Another alarming trend is the movement to "push down" the first-grade curriculum into kindergarten and sometimes even to the nursery school. Behind this movement is the idea that four- and five-year-olds should not "waste" these early years learning to love books, explore the world around them, solve problems, learn about their own capabilities, and learn how to get along with their peers. Their time, it is thought, should be spent in more "academic" pursuits.

Related to the "push down" curriculum is the trend for all-day kindergartens and the expectation that every minute be spent in academic pursuits. Five-year-olds may be excited about riding the big yellow school bus with their lunch box in hand to spend the whole day, but how many have the energy level and attention span to spend all day in academic pursuits?

It is not only the hours spent in school devoted to academic achievement, it is also the hours after school in such organized activities as ballet lessons, music lessons, karate lessons, swim and gym classes, art classes, and computer classes that fill the afternoons of young children. Is the neighborhood game of kickball no longer an acceptable pastime? Is playing dress-up no longer looked on with favor? Our attitudes about what is important for young children to know and to do seem to be changing. Attitudes about children's leisure time are changing. Must children always be in some sort of scheduled activity? Whatever became of free play?

These are some of the real issues creating the tumultuous state of education for our young children. How do we respond to these issues in our early childhood education programs? What kind of learning climate do we need in early childhood classrooms? In the next chapter, let us look at the multifaceted entity known as learning climate.

A Learning Climate for Young Children

A positive learning climate in a school is a composite of many things. It is an attitude that respects children. It is a place where children receive guidance and encouragement from the responsible adults around them. It is an environment where children can experiment and try out new ideas without fear of failure. It is an atmosphere that builds children's self-confidence so they dare to take risks. It is an environment that nurtures a love of learning.

A positive learning climate must be a safe place. Children's physical safety must be a primary concern in the classroom. This means the equipment they use in the classroom and on the playground must be in good repair. For the children, safety means having rules about what is permissible and what is not. Safety means being aware of one's own body and physical movements within the classroom space. Safety means being sensitive to other people and how they should be treated.

A positive classroom climate is one in which children feel as comfortable as they feel at home. They should feel comfortable about moving around the classroom with ease. They should feel comfortable about expressing their thoughts freely, without fear of ridicule.

In a positive classroom climate, the curriculum includes activities that are relevant to the lives of young children, with opportunities to work individually, in small groups, or as a total class. These activities are organized around interest areas, such as blockbuilding, science and art projects, dramatic play, manipulatives, music, and storytelling. All these activities take place in an unpressured atmosphere.

In a positive classroom climate, learning occurs through the active exploration of materials, through interaction with other children and the teacher. Learning involves both materials and people.

The Teacher's Role in Creating a Positive Learning Climate

The teacher has many roles in creating a stimulating learning environment in the classroom, beginning with an attitude of respect for each child's interests, abilities, maturation level, and learning style. The teacher works to develop children's self-esteem by seeing that each child has many successes. Praise for each success generates more success. The teacher provides many opportunities for decision making so that children can work out problems among themselves as much as possible. By working together to solve problems, young children gain practice in many social skills.

The teacher stimulates children's language development by having them listen to and dictate stories, by having them listen to and learn songs, by providing them with engaging props for dramatic play in the housekeeping corner, and by using new vocabulary as they make and bake pumpkin bread. Children are introduced to the written language as they come to recognize their name above their cubby and their classmates' names on the "juice and cracker" chart. Children learn to express themselves as they meet with their teacher each morning to discuss the day's activities, to share their observations about the toad in the classroom terrarium, or to express their concern about a problem at home. By listening and by asking questions about the world around them, children become more and more proficient in communicating.

The teacher provides activities each day to foster small muscle development. By having available puzzles, scissors, design cubes, and all sorts of manipulatives and by encouraging and guiding children in their use, the teacher is helping children develop their small muscle coordination. At the same time, the teacher allows children the freedom to use their bodies and voices in vigorous outdoor activities. Children need a time for rough-and-tumble play (within the limits of safety) and a time to be noisy.

The teacher creates a classroom environment that is aesthetically satisfying. This includes not only providing experiences in music and art but also choosing materials and decorating the room in ways that are aesthetically pleasing. Aesthetics should pervade the classroom environment, from the pictures displayed on the wall to the selection of neckties in the housekeeping corner. Aesthetics should be a factor in decisions about the equipment and materials children use. By constantly surrounding young children with beauty, they gradually develop aesthetic judgment.

A teacher conveys to children and their parents that the play-like activities of early childhood are really work, and that enjoying the process of work is essential for living. Doing a wooden puzzle of a nurse holding two newborn babies is play. It is also work. Building the George Washington Bridge with wooden blocks is play. It is also work. Making a gallon of orange juice from a quart of concentrate for mid-morning snack is play. It is also work. Everything that goes on in an early childhood classroom may appear to be play, but it is a way of learning, a way of growing. It is a process called work. To be able to enjoy this process is what early childhood education is all about.

In a positive learning climate, a teacher enjoys the company of young children. She can laugh each time Howie tells a silly knock-knock joke. She reminds David of past successes when nothing seems to be going right for him. She is a nurse for Jennifer who scratched her finger on the climbing bars, but encourages her to try the bars again. The teacher makes her room a place where a young child wants to be, a place where people can talk to one another, comfort one another, plan with one another, and work things out together. A teacher enjoys the company of young children because each and every one of them is a worthwhile human being.

In a positive learning climate, the teacher is a good listener, a good observer, and a good recorder. Her ears and eyes are constantly attuned to the happenings around her. She makes a notation in her individual record file that on October 5, Charlotte and Rachel, both of whom have trouble establishing relationships with other children, took each other's hand out on the playground and talked to one another. This could be the beginning of a budding friendship. Perhaps a note or phone call to Charlotte's and Rachel's mothers would be in order, with the suggestion that they arrange for the two girls to play together after school.

A teacher of young children can laugh at herself and admit her own mistakes. Nothing is quite as hilarious to a four-year-old as a teacher spilling paint on the floor or forgetting how to pronounce the name of the long-necked, plant-eating dinosaur. Young children need to know that grown-ups are not perfect, that they can make mistakes just like a four-year-old, and the world will not come to an end.

A teacher of young children is an ongoing learner, just like the children in the classroom. She is excited about discovering something different and conveys this excitement to the children. When she and the children discover a strange new insect in a rotting tree trunk in the woods, she puts it in a plastic container in her pocket. Then, back in the classroom, they look in the insect book and try to identify the strange new creature. A teacher of young children learns from nature, from books, from other teachers, and from the children. She models for the children that learning new things is an important part of her life.

Finally, a teacher of young children helps children to say goodbye and look forward to the new experience of another school and another teacher. She tells the class that she will miss each and every one of them and lets them know they are always welcome to return to visit, just like Jeannette did on Columbus Day. She writes a letter to Sam telling him how many toads she found in her garden over the summer. She asks David to call her on the phone this summer and tell her about his soccer playing at day camp. Young children need to know that friendships can continue, even though they are going on to a different school with a different teacher.

These are some of the roles a teacher can play in creating a rich and nurturing climate for learning.

The First Few Days of School: Making the Transition

The first few days of school are a critical period for establishing a positive classroom climate for young children. Some children will make the transition from home to school much more easily than others. Parents need to understand this and not feel that they have somehow failed if their child has difficulty separating from them. (Sometimes the separation is as difficult for the parents as it is for their child.) Children are different. Children's needs are different. Parents are asked to stay at school during the first few days.

Ask the parents to bring a book to read or handwork to do. Have them sit down in a part of room where they are in view of their child but not intruding on the child's activities. Just being there is reassuring to the child who is upset. Later, as the activities get under way, the parents can go to the teachers' lounge for coffee or tea but are "on call" if the teacher wants them back in the classroom. In the lounge they can meet other parents, discuss mutual interests, and perhaps develop new friendships.

One way of easing young children into the routine of school is to start gradually. Make the first two days of school two hour-long sessions, the third day two hours long, and after that run the full schedule. Have only half the class come the first hour, and the remainder come for the second hour for the first two days. With only half the class present, the noise level is greatly reduced and the teacher can give more individual attention to the children. With only half the class, it is easier for Jon to learn everyone's name, and Joanna doesn't have to wait so long to hold the guinea pig.

Creating a Positive Climate in the Classroom

The classroom is a child's home away from home. The single most important job for the teacher of young children is to create a homelike environment within the classroom so that all children feel comfortable to explore, to test themselves, and to work out their problems both large and small.

The classroom should be divided into clearly defined learning areas, which give children an immediate sense of order when they enter the room. A sense of order is reassuring to children. They quickly learn that some places are for quiet activities and other places are for more active pursuits. It is equally important that children learn that they have a role in maintaining the order in the classroom. Order can help a child to learn.

One learning area is the science corner. This is the place where children observe and handle animals. It is a place to learn how to care for various creatures in the classroom menagerie, a place to ask questions. For Debbie, it is the place to work up the courage to pick up a red eft and let it walk ever so gently across the palm of her hand. It is the place where Jeffrey can sit in the rocking chair and feed the guinea pig a string bean and brush him lovingly. The science corner is a comfortable place for young children to explore the world of nature.

Another learning area is the library corner. It is a place with a carpet on the floor and a bookcase filled with wonderful children's classics like *Caps for Sale* or *The Story of Ferdinand* and also lesser-known favorites like *Good Dog, Carl,* and *Owly*. These are books to enjoy listening to while curled up on the teacher's lap or sitting next to her. These are books to look at by yourself propped up against a big throw pillow or sprawled out on the carpet. These are stories to hear over and over again. This is a place to dream, a place to be alone, a place to share a conversation with a new-found friend. The library corner is a comfortable place for young children to learn about the world of books.

Still another learning area is the housekeeping corner, sometimes called the dress-up corner. This is a place for dramatic play. Here one might find a policeman's hat, an engineer's cap, and a construction worker's hardhat. There are flashy flowered ties, a bright red vest, and workmen's boots. There are silver high-heeled shoes, a pink flowered hat, rhinestone necklaces, and a rainbow of plastic bracelets. There is a child-sized chest of drawers with bow ties and wrist watches that no longer tell the correct time. There are bristle shaving brushes, an embroidered pocketbook, which has seen better days, and bunches of keys. There is a table covered with a red-and-white checked cloth and three spindle-back chairs to sit on. There are bright, primary color plastic dishes and cutlery. There are empty cans of Davis Baking Powder and Campbell's Chunky Chicken Noodle Soup. There are irons and telephones. There are boy and girl baby dolls nestled together in a small wooden bed under a pale yellow blanket. There are so many things in the dress-up corner to engage young children's imaginations to go shopping, to cook dinner, to take care of the babies, or to go to work. The props are there and so is the rich fantasy life of young children. The dress-up corner is a comfortable place for young children's dramatic play.

Art activities are a basic component of the early childhood curriculum. Each day when the children arrive at school, materials for an art project are laid out on the table. No formal art instruction is offered, but the teacher is there to help when needed. The materials themselves are enough to capture the attention of the young artists, and they eagerly proceed to use them for a variety of projects. Often an art project is repeated a second day for those who were engaged in another activity or for those who want to try a variation of what they did the day before.

Three or four easels for painting are essential equipment for the early childhood classroom. Each is covered with fresh sheets of newspaper each day along with a large piece of white painting paper. The childen wear plastic smocks so they can work freely without concern for spilling paint on their clothes. Working with the thick tempera paint and a large brush is a relaxing activity for young children and allows them to express their deepest thoughts and feelings.

Displaying children's finished art projects is a way of telling them that their work is valued. The displays also serve as a reminder to children who have not yet done an art project or painting that they, too, can create beautiful things. The art table and easels are places of comfort, places to experiment and to let the imagination soar.

Another vital activity in the early childhood classroom is blockbuilding. Having a large supply of different sized blocks offers limitless possibilities for individual and group construction projects. Blockbuilding is an open-ended activity; there are no right or wrong ways to make a construction. Children, without knowing it, are learning to work out mathematical problems. When working on a group construction, they are learning to work out social relationships. Perhaps more than any other medium, blockbuilding offers children an outlet for creative expression.

Safety is an important consideration in blockbuilding activity. A few rules are necessary, rules that allow for freedom within a given structure. The following rules are some the author has found useful in her classes:

1. Hardhats must be worn if the building you are constructing is taller than you are or if you are working within tumbling distance of another building that is taller than you are.

2. Blocks are not to be stepped on because someone might slip and fall.
3. Blocks are not to be dropped from a height because it may cause them to splinter.
4. Blocks are not to be taken from another person's building without permission.
5. When block constructions are taken down, they are "unbuilt" from the top down.
6. Block constructions are not to be crashed to the floor.

Sometimes it will be necessary to leave a block building up overnight so the young architect can continue the project the next day. Also, taking photographs of a block construction and its builder with an instant camera is a good way to preserve the memory of a well-executed building project.

The learning and activity areas described in this chapter create the climate in which young children can develop socially, physically, emotionally, and intellectually. It is an orderly climate, yet one that allows for choice, freedom, and creativity. It is a comfortable climate for young children.

The Classroom Out-of-Doors

The outside play area is as much a part of the early childhood curriculum as the classroom is. And it deserves the same consideration when it comes to creating a climate for learning. The classroom ground rules for safety and comfort should apply equally to the out-of-doors.

Children need to know that their teacher is nearby looking out for their welfare at all times. Sometimes a teacher needs to remind Betty that she will get a better grip on the climbing bars if she takes her mittens off. Sometimes the teacher needs to remind Harvey that there must be one-way traffic on the slide. There are times when rough-and-tumble play goes over the edge, and you have to say, "Stop, you're getting too rough. I want you to think about what else you can do on the playground."

Outdoor playground equipment may also involve safety factors, but more important are the different ways equipment can be used to develop coordination and to give children confidence in their abilities. A word of encouragement and two helping hands may be necessary when Matthew wants to drop to the ground from the horizontal ladder. Jane may work up the courage to try hanging by her knees by watching Donna do it. However, children must not be pushed into physical feats until they feel ready for them. Skills of strength and coordination develop gradually and at different rates in young children.

The outdoor curriculum can extend to nearby woods and meadows. In the woods children can turn over rotting tree trunks to look for wire worms and potato bugs. They can look for yellow-spotted salamanders living underneath the stones. They can look for birds with the "binoculars" they have made out of two painted toilet tissue rolls glued together and a yarn strap. In the woods they can stop and listen to the strident call of the blue jay or the resonant tapping of the downy woodpecker searching for insects on a tree trunk. In the woods children can mark their trail with pieces of red yarn and then delight in retracing their steps by following their markers. Children should walk in the woods in the fall and the spring to see the changes that nature brings with the seasons. The woods are full of things to be discovered. The woods are an exciting and comfortable place for young children.

School Climate and Staff Interaction

A vital component of the learning climate of a school is how the staff interact with one another. Whatever the early childhood setting — private nursery school, Head Start, day care, or public school — children are like barometers, reflecting the moods and attitudes of the adults around them. When a staff works together harmoniously, the children have a sense of "family" and respond accordingly. When there is disharmony, children sense the tension and respond accordingly.

Teachers can learn much from one another. Being able to visit other classrooms, even for a short period, can give a teacher insight into how to deal with a particular situation or to learn about a new class project. Staff meetings also can be a time for sharing ideas. One meeting might focus on a particular child. It is often helpful to hear from the teacher who had the child in her class the previous year. Another meeting might focus on art projects or science experiments that the children enjoyed. Of equal importance is discussion of projects that were not well received or did not come off as expected. There is much to be gained in sharing the negative as well as the positive.

Teachers can share ideas. They can share materials. They can share things that the class has made with other children in the school. It takes only a little extra effort to make a larger bowl of applesauce or a second loaf of pumpkin bread. Sharing good things the children have helped to make sets an example for sharing other good things in their lives. Teachers also can share with each other something of their lives outside the school setting. Getting to know colleagues on a more personal level can lead to lifelong friendships.

Another form of sharing are those times when all the children, staff, and sometimes whole families come together for joyful school events. Just as families come together for celebrations, so should the entire student body gather to gain a sense of belonging. It might be the weekly meeting for singing, where the children learn new songs like "Pussywillow" or sing old favorites like "Five Green and Speckled Frogs" accompanied by the autoharp. It might be the annual school fair, which the parents organize and run as a fund-raiser. The children take great pride in having their mommies or daddies involved. Enthusiasm builds as the fair date approaches. The children talk about last year's fair, the proceeds of which were used to purchase a new piece of playground equipment. It is more than a school fair; it is a family fair. It might be the school picnic on the last day of school with blankets spread out on the playground. These all are memorable occasions in the lives of young children. They are part of the nurturing climate of a school, which the staff creates cooperatively.

The director or principal of the school also plays an important role in creating a positive climate for young children and their parents. This role involves spending a lot of time in classrooms and becoming familiar with all the children, with their progress and with their problems. It involves planning meaningful parent meetings and bringing in resource speakers to discuss child development and other aspects of early childhood education. It involves providing support to the staff with educational materials, with sharing expertise on modes of discipline or ways of working with a difficult parent. The director or principal orchestrates the climate of a school and sees to it that every player is heard.

Working with Parents to Create a Positive Learning Climate

The teacher of young children can begin to establish a climate for learning even before the school doors open in the fall. The method is simple: a home visit to each child in the incoming class. Much can be learned in a home visit that will influence how a teacher approaches the first days of school with a child. And just the fact of taking the time and effort to make a home visit communicates to children and their parents that the teacher cares about them.

Home visits should be made by appointment at the convenience of the parents a week or two before the opening of school. The visits need not be long; 20 to 30 minutes is usually sufficient. Some time should be spent listening and responding to parents' questions and comments, but most of the time should be devoted to finding out the child's interests or favorite activities.

At school the classroom is the center of the child's world. At home the bedroom is the child's private world. In it you gain glimpses and insights into the things the child holds dear. It might be an often-hugged brown teddy bear nestled in Sarah's pillow. It might be a shoe box filled with treasured stones and shells Rebecca collected on the beach at Fire Island. In some homes you will see a child's bedroom so filled with toys that there is little room to move. In other homes you will see a child's bedroom devoid of books, puzzles, dolls, stuffed animals, trucks, or blocks − devoid of any signs of childhood.

Visiting a child's bedroom can tell you a lot. Make it an intimate time; sit on the floor to chat with the child or to play a game. You might find that Robert is a past master at playing Fish. This is the child's initial school contact. It is a time to communicate some of the excitement of the days ahead. The home visit establishes a climate of expectation.

Parent Orientation

After the home visit, the next time the parents and the teacher meet is at parent orientation. This, too, is a part of the climate the teacher must create for the early childhood years. It is the time when the teacher presents general information about school procedures. It is a time for the teacher to share something about herself — a person in whom parents have placed custody of their children for several hours each day. And most important, it is a time to explain to parents the educational philosophy guiding the early childhood curriculum.

When the parents arrive, the classroom is already set up for opening day. The parents can see their child's name on a sign over the cubby that will hold their child's belongings. They can see the materials their child will be using and the activity centers where their child will play (work). Parents are given name tags and invited to partake of a cup of coffee, tea, or cider while the group gathers.

Each set of parents receives an emergency card to fill out listing the name and phone number of mother, father, guardian, pediatrician, and other close friend or relative to contact if the parent cannot be reached. A telephone directory is available to look up numbers if necessary. Parents are also given a medical release form to sign. Other materials provided are a school list with names, addresses, and phone numbers of all children, their parents, and school staff and a sheet with carpool regulations. Each set of forms distributed has the child's last name clearly printed in the left-hand corner. The medical examination and personal history forms have already been sent to parents by mail.

Other procedures explained are the extra clothing children need to have at school, the requirement of a note or phone call if a child is going home with another child, policies regarding birthday celebrations in the classroom, and such miscellaneous items as sending the guinea pig or other classroom pets home with one child each weekend. After all procedural matters are covered, the teacher then devotes the rest of the orientation to a discussion of her educational philosophy for young children.

Parents come to the orientation session with varying expectations for their child's first school experience. The orientation is an ideal time to present the goals of the early childhood curriculum and how the school goes about achieving them. For example, parents need to understand that activities start at a simple level and become more complex as the year progresses. This is true with the stories that are read, the art projects that are constructed, and the cooking products that are made. As children's attention span increases and they master simple skills, they can move on to more complex activities. In all the children's activities, the emphasis is on the process not the product. The goal is to have the children enjoy the process of work, whether it is painting a picture or building the World Trade Center in the block corner.

Another important goal of the early childhood curriculum is developing decision making. It may be Gina deciding which color to use for painting a picture of her sister Ava, or James deciding whether to take a fifth Hi-Ho cracker at snacktime, when he knows he is allowed only four. Both are important decisions for a four- or five-year-old. It is deciding whether to help Erica pick up the 56 mealworms that spilled on the floor or deciding whether to put your arm around Masakuni's shoulder because he's crying so hard for his mommy. Both are important decisions.

Children need time in which to work out decisions, time to sort things out, time to think things through. Gina needs to hear a voice of approval when she has decided to paint her sister Ava's dress a delectable blue. James needs to hear a voice of approval when he has just counted out four Hi-Ho crackers for his snack. All the children need to hear that it was really helpful of Alexis to stop doing the wooden farm puzzle in order to help Erica pick up the 56 mealworms. They need to hear that it was helpful for Anne to put her arm around Masakuni's shoulder to comfort him.

Still another goal of the early childhood curriculum is developing respect for self and others. In order for this to happen, the teacher must want it to happen. She must respect each child's individual differences, each child's emerging self. She must listen to the children's collective heartbeat, empathize with their problems and frustrations, and at the same time, provide them with opportunities that challenge them to grow.

In turn, the children must respect the teacher, but this does not occur automatically. It is earned. It is earned by listening and then acting on what has been heard. It is earned by being fair to each child. It is earned by being consistent day after day throughout the school year. Respect for each child grows out of one's own self-respect. A teacher expecting to see these qualities in each child must first see them in herself.

Finally, parents should understand the importance of communicating to the teacher any information that is relevant to the child's welfare. The teacher needs to know if there is sickness or a death in the family, or if mommy or daddy is away on an extended business trip. The teacher needs to know that the morning got off to a bad start for Melanie, because in the carpool Charlie said he wasn't going to be her best friend anymore. The teacher needs to know what incidents may be affecting a child's behavior in school on a particular day. Then she can talk about it with the child, provide that extra bit of support, and maybe make allowances for the child's participation in the scheduled activities for the day.

This writer, in her parent orientation, concludes the session by reading a selection from her book, *Teaching Four-Year-Olds: A Personal Journey* (Phi Delta Kappa Educational Foundation, 1989), titled "The Hidden Curriculum." Readers who agree with the points of view expressed in this selection are invited to use it or an adaptation of it with their own parent orientation sessions.

The Hidden Curriculum

When someone asks me what I do, and I answer that I am a teacher of four-year-olds, I sometimes get the response: "What on earth can you teach them?" Many years ago I would have answered by describing some of the science projects or work with art materials I did with children. Now it is different: I feel more secure in my own position; I tell them what I really do. I teach children about the world they live in, about themselves and their peers. And I teach children about adults, trust, and love. I work with attitudes. I hope to inspire a love of learning. This is what I teach.

I want to know each child like I know the back of my hand. I want to recognize their voices from across the room so if I'm busy tying Sarah's shoes, I can answer without looking up. I want to know their wardrobes so I can recognize a new pair of shoelaces or a new barrette when it is worn for the first time. I want to know what gives them pleasure and makes them smile. I want to know what really irritates them or makes them sad. I want to know what books they like to look at and what they like to eat. I want to know their favorite colors and their favorite stuffed animal. I want to know what scares them and what tickles their funny bone. I want to be able to read their eyes so I can tell if their day has not started well. I want to know a lot of things. And I want them to know I know.

I want children to know themselves and feel good about what they know. I want children to recognize that there are areas in which they need to grow. I want children to learn to express themselves, but I accept the fact that some are not able to do that yet and are still fighting the world with their fists. I want children to come to terms with themselves, whatever those terms may be. I want to help each child accomplish these things through my caring.

I want children to respect each other for what they are. I want children to know that, although there are differences among them, these differences are what make each of them unique persons. I want them to know that people can change and that they all can help to make positive changes happen. I want them to know that we all have feelings and that each of us can feel hurt. And I want them to know how it feels to help another person.

I want children to know their teacher, to know her as a friend. I want children to know that adults are there to help them grow, to set limits, and to protect them. I want children to know that when they are sad or troubled, there is always a lap for them to climb on and receive comfort.

I want children to know that nursery school is now a big part of their world and that they are an important part of this world. I want children to know that this is where they are supposed to be and that Mommy and Daddy want them to be here. I want children to know that next year they will be in a different place and that they will be ready to leave here and move on to kindergarten. This is what I teach. This is the hidden curriculum.

By helping parents to understand all the elements that go into the learning climate of the early childhood classroom, the teacher is developing the home-school cooperation needed to build and maintain this climate.

The Parent Conference

Regularly scheduled parent conferences are an important aspect of school climate for young children. Some schools schedule three: one about six weeks after school begins, one mid-year, and a third close to the end of the year. In some cases, additional conferences will be necessary when dealing with a specific child's problem.

The initial conference is primarily a listening time for the teachers. We want parents to tell us what their child is saying about school, what he or she likes or doesn't like about school. We want parents to tell us what they want the school year to bring for their child. We want to tell the parents what our goals are. We want them to know that we want to work together.

In addition to scheduled conferences are the notes and phone calls to and from parents and the informal moments on the playground or waiting for the car pool. These are the occasions for telling a parent that Thomas constructed his first skyscraper with blocks and was most pleased with the results, or that Gabrielle seemed lethargic, not her usual self. These simple comments convey to parents that the teacher is there for both their children and for them.

Conclusion

The education of our young children is in a tumultuous state. Despite the pressures imposed by society on children and their families, teachers must create a positive climate in which young children can learn and grow.

A positive school climate begins with that first telephone call to parents to set up an appointment for the home visit. It is saying that we are interested in their child and the things their child holds dear. It is saying that we want to know their child so we can plan the kinds of experiences that will build on what the parents have done at home.

A positive school climate is reflected in the way we set up the classroom for a rich and varied curriculum that is appropriate for the developmental level of young children. The positive climate pervades everything that transpires in the classroom, the way the teacher reacts to and interacts with the children and the way children interact with each other.

A positive school climate is reflected in the way the staff work together; the way they share ideas, materials, and experiences; the way they cooperate on all-school activities that all the children enjoy.

A positive school climate nurtures children, parents, and teachers. Above all, a positive school climate nurtures the love of learning.